HEALTHY IN A HURRY: SMOOTHIE RECIPE

CONTENTS

SMOOTHIES

- FRUITS & SPINACH SMOOTHIE ....
- DELICIOUS BEET SMOOTHIE 9
- CREAMY CHOCOLATE AVOCADO SMOOTHIE 10
- WONDERFUL WATERMELON SMOOTHIE 11
- CRANBERRY AND ORANGE SMOOTHIE 12
- BANANA & PEANUT BUTTER SMOOTHIE 13
- YUMMY CHERRY & ALMOND SMOOTHIE 14
- SPINACH & BROCCOLI SMOOTHIE 15
- GREEN GRAPE SMOOTHIE 16
- SO PEACHY SMOOTHIE 17
- PINEAPPLE-KIWI SMOOTHIE 18
- BEST PUMPKIN SMOOTHIE 19
- BERRY BANANA SMOOTHIE 20
- YUMMY PAPAYA SMOOTHIE 21
- REFRESHING CUCUMBER SMOOTHIE 22
- CARROT AND RASPBERRY SMOOTHIE 23
- SUPER POWERED SMOOTHIE 24
- GRAPE APPLE SMOOTHIE 25
- DELICIOUS PEAR SMOOTHIE 26
- VERY BERRY KALE SMOOTHIE 27
- CANTALOUPE SMOOTHIE 28
- ZUCCHINI SUMMER SMOOTHIE 29
- THE TOMATO SMOOTHIE 30
- DELICIOUS DATE SMOOTHIE 31
- GINGER & BANANA SMOOTHIE 32
- DREAMY ORANGE SMOOTHIE 33
- BERRY, BANANA & SOY SMOOTHIE 34
- APRICOT & MANGO SMOOTHIE 35
- RADISH & FRUIT SMOOTHIE 36
- BLACKBERRY SMOOTHIE 37
- ACAI & CHERRY SMOOTHIE 38
- SWEET POTATO SMOOTHIE 39
- PEACHY COCONUT SMOOTHIE 40
- PEANUT BUTTER & BANANA SMOOTHIE 41
- SIMPLE PEAR SMOOTHIE 42
- PLUM SMOOTHIE 43
- KICK START GRAPEFRUIT SMOOTHIE 44
- LIME & LEMON DETOX SMOOTHIE 45

- Rolled Oats Smoothie 46
- Dark Chocolate Smoothie 47
- Almond and Apple Smoothie 48
- Christmas Smoothie 49
- Sweet Macadamia Smoothie 50
- Energy Booster Smoothie 51
- Brazil Smoothie 52
- Fruity Tofu Smoothie 53
- Dragon Fruit Smoothie 54
- Kid's Smoothie Pop 55
- Hazelnut and Chocolate Smoothie 56
- Peachy Spinach Smoothie 57

GRANOLA 59
- Homemade Granola 59
- Awesome Applesauce Granola 61
- Nuts & Coconut Granola 62
- Chunky Chow Granola 63
- Crunchy Cranberry Granola 64

BARS & COOKIES 66
- Chewy Date and Cranberry Bars 66
- Microwave Breakfast Squares 67
- No Bake Bars 68
- Peanut Butter Bars 69
- Almond Coconut Bars 70
- Marvelous Molasses Bars 71
- Cinnamon Granola Bars 72
- Gluten Free Bars 73
- Granola Energy Balls 74
- Easy Pumpkin Seed Bars 75
- Awesome Apricot Bars 76
- Kid's Favorite Breakfast Bars 77
- Nutty Energy Bar 78
- Chocolate and Peanut Bar 79
- Chewy Fruity & Nutty Bars 80
- Poppin Popcorn Bars 81
- Healthy Banana Nut Cookies 82
- Morning Cookies 83
- Easy Oatmeal Banana Cookies 85
- Super Charged Breakfast Cookies 86
- Nutty Morning Cookies 87
- Sunshine Pumpkin Cookies 88

Healthy in a Hurry

Smoothie Recipes, Breakfast Bars and Grab & Go Snacks

Elizabeth Greenway

ELIZABETH GREENWAY

Copyright © 2014 Elizabeth Greenway

All rights reserved.

ISBN-13: 978-1503244122

MUFFINS 90
FIBER RICH MUFFINS 90
GOOD MORNING MUFFINS 91
PLENTY SWEET TRAIL MIX 92
DRIED CHERRY MUFFINS 93
CINNAMON & APPLE MUFFINS 94
PINEAPPLE & PAPAYA MUFFINS 95
YUMMY PECAN PIE MUFFINS 96
MINIATURE BANANA MUFFINS 97
CHRISTMAS CRANBERRY MUFFINS 98
EASY OATMEAL MUFFINS 99
NUTTY COCONUT & APPLE MUFFINS 100
CARROT MUFFINS 101
SWEET PUMPKIN MINI MUFFINS 102

TRAIL MIX & PARTY MIX 104
TRAVELING TRAIL MIX 104
SUPER CRUNCHY TRAIL MIX 105
LUNCH BOX TRAIL MIX 106
SPICED UP TRAIL MIX 107
SO-GOOD PARTY MIX 108
SWEET AND SALTY TRAIL MIX 109
NEW ORLEANS PARTY MIX 110
KIDDO'S TRAIL MIX 111
HAPPY HOLIDAY PARTY MIX 112
HAUNTED HALLOWEEN PARTY MIX 113

Healthy in a Hurry

The smoothie is one of the few food items that not only tastes delicious but is also chunk full of healthy nutrients. Originating in the 1930's, the smoothie started out as nothing more than a piece of fruit, ice and some fruit juice. Today there are all sorts of combinations of yogurts, milks, fruits, nuts, veggies, seeds and more that make up a smoothie.

This hearty daily drink is chunk full of vitamins, minerals and antioxidants required to keep our bodies and minds functioning at their utmost best. There is simply no better way to obtain healthy nutrients than with a smoothie consisting of vegetables, fruits and other beneficial ingredients.

All that's required to create the smoothies in this book is a good blender and the listed ingredients. You can add or take away for any smoothie recipe just by adjusting its liquid content. Also, ice or frozen fruit can be added if you desire a colder drink. Each recipe has a brief health benefit of at least one of the ingredients to help in deciding which smoothie is best suited for you or a loved one.

Whether it's for the yummy flavor, health benefits or both, you are sure to enjoy the smoothies and grab-and-go snacks in this cookbook.

SMOOTHIES

Fruits & Spinach Smoothie

The tropical pineapple is rich in vitamins A and C, calcium, phosphorus, and potassium, so drink up.

1 1/2 cups fresh spinach

1 ripe banana

1 cup frozen or fresh blueberries (set aside a few blueberries for garnish)

1/2 cup plain or vanilla yogurt

1/4 cup fresh pineapple

1/4 cup frozen cherries

1/4 cup orange juice

Place all the ingredients into a blender and blend until smooth. Pour smoothie into glass and top with a few blueberries.

Delicious Beet Smoothie

Beets are a high source of energy, have loads of vitamins and minerals plus are known to be a natural aphrodisiac... who knew?

1 gala apple, diced

1/2 cup raw beets, diced

1/2 cup frozen berry mix

1/2 cup orange juice

1 to 1/2 inch fresh ginger, sliced thin

1/4 cup soy or almond milk

Juice from 1 lime

1 teaspoon agave

3 ice cubes

Fresh mint (for garnish)

Place all the ingredients except for the fresh mint into a blender and blend until smooth. Pour into glass and garnish with fresh mint if desired.

Creamy Chocolate Avocado Smoothie

The avocado has numerous health benefits such as promotes eye health, protects against cancer, a natural anti-inflammatory and many more.

2 tablespoons dark chocolate chips

1 ripe avocado, peeled and pitted

3 tablespoons honey

3 tablespoons unsweetened cocoa powder

2 cups vanilla flavored almond milk

1 tablespoon vanilla extract

13 ice cubes

Place all the ingredients into a blender and blend until thick and creamy. Pour into glass and garnish top with a few chocolate chips.

Wonderful Watermelon Smoothie

Watermelon is good for the heart as it improves blood circulation, relaxes blood vessels plus it is rich in vitamins A & C.

2 cups watermelon, diced

1/2 cup ice or frozen watermelon

Juice from half of a lime

2 lime slices (for garnish)

Place all the ingredients into a blender and blend until smooth. Pour into glass and place a sliced lime on the rim for an attractive and delicious summer time drink.

Cranberry and Orange Smoothie

Cranberries are high in antioxidants which help strengthen the immune system and helps keep you looking young both inside and out.

1 1/4 cups vanilla Greek yogurt

1 cup orange juice

1/2 cup pure cranberry juice

1/2 teaspoon honey

1/2 teaspoon cinnamon

1/2 cup crushed ice

Place all the ingredients into a blender and blend until smooth. Pour into a glass and garnish with a slice of orange on the rim if desired.

Banana & Peanut Butter Smoothie

Peanut butter has magnesium for healthy bones, potassium for healthy muscles and vitamin B6 for a strong immune system.

2/3 cup almond milk

1/2 cup Greek vanilla yogurt

1 large frozen sliced banana

1 tablespoon peanut butter

2 cups fresh baby spinach

Place all the ingredients into a blender and blend until smooth. Pour into a glass and place a few chopped peanuts and banana on top, so delicious!

Yummy Cherry & Almond Smoothie

Cherries aren't just delicious; they help fight cancer, ease arthritis pain, help you sleep and aid in lowering blood pressure and more.

1/2 cup almond milk

1/2 cup plain Greek yogurt

1/2 cup dark frozen cherries

1 tablespoon honey

1/2 teaspoon almond extract

Place all the ingredients into a blender and blend until smooth. Pour into glass then add crushed almonds on top if desired.

Spinach & Broccoli Smoothie

Broccoli is high in vitamin C, has high levels of calcium and vitamin K which help prevent osteoporosis.

1 chopped apple

1 cup fresh spinach

1 chopped carrot

2 peeled oranges, quartered

4 florets of broccoli

1/2 cup or less of water

Place all the ingredients into a blender and blend until smooth. Pour into a glass with a slice of orange placed on the rim.

Green Grape Smoothie

The delicious green grape is ripe with vitamins C and K, has minerals such as potassium and iron to help promote a strong heart, now isn't that sweet.

1 chopped granny smith apple

1 cup baby spinach, packed

3 cups frozen green grapes, remove stems

1 1/2 cups of apple juice

Place all the ingredients into a blender and blend until smooth. Pour into glass and garnish with a slice of lime on the rim for an enticing warm weather drink.

So Peachy Smoothie

Llycopene and lutein found in peaches helps to prevent macular degeneration and cancer. Now that's a peach.

2 cups of soy or almond milk

2 1/2 cups frozen sliced peaches

2 tablespoons honey or sugar

5 ice cubes

Mint leafs (for garnish)

Place all the ingredients into a blender and blend until smooth. Pour into glass and garnish with mint leafs.

Pineapple-Kiwi Smoothie

The little kiwi fruit is big in improving digestive health, boosting the immunity system and weight loss.

1 ripe banana, sliced

1/4 cup pineapple, chopped

1 cup peeled kiwi fruit, sliced

2 cups baby spinach

1/2 cup plain yogurt

1/2 cup orange juice

2 tablespoons chia seeds or flaxseed meal

Place all the ingredients into a blender and blend until smooth. Pour into glass and top with diced kiwi or pineapple if desired.

Best Pumpkin Smoothie

Fiber rich pumpkin aids in promoting weight loss, plus it's a great source of beta-carotene which is beneficial to your eyesight and skin.

1/2 cup canned pumpkin

3/4 cup plain or vanilla yogurt

2 teaspoons brown sugar

1/4 teaspoon ground cinnamon

1/8 teaspoon nutmeg

4 to 5 ice cubes

Whip cream (for garnish)

Place all the ingredients into a blender and blend until smooth. Pour into glass, garnish with a dollop of whipped cream sprinkled with a little brown sugar.

Berry Banana Smoothie

Rich in potassium, vitamin B6, fiber, magnesium and vitamin C, it's no wonder the banana is one of nature's healthiest prepackaged foods; not just for monkeys.

1 ripe banana, sliced

5 strawberries, sliced

1 cup mixed frozen berries

1 1/4 cup orange or pineapple juice

Place all the ingredients into a blender and blend until smooth. Pour into glass and place a slice of strawberry on the rim.

Yummy Papaya Smoothie

The delicious papaya has a long list of health and beauty benefits such as it aids in digestion, promotes healthy looking skin, and helps heal wounds and more.

2 3/4 cups papaya, chopped

2/3 cup plain yogurt

1 tablespoon fresh ginger, thinly sliced

Juice from 2 lemons

1 tablespoon honey

1 cup ice

Mint leaves (for garnish)

Place all the ingredients into a blender and blend until smooth. Pour into glass and garnish with mint leaves.

Refreshing Cucumber Smoothie

Cucumbers have potassium, vitamin C, K, B1, manganese, molybdenum, magnesium, biotin and more; no wonder the cucumber is one of the healthiest foods you can eat.

1 cucumber, diced

2 cups cantaloupe, diced

1 cup red watermelon, diced

1 teaspoon lime juice

2 cups fresh baby spinach

1/2 cup cold water

Place all the ingredients into a blender and blend until smooth. Pour into glass and if desired garnish with a sliced cucumber on the rim.

Carrot and Raspberry Smoothie

The raspberry is high in anti-oxidants, is an excellent source of vitamin C and B complex, plus they are low in calories, so drink up!

3 cups frozen raspberries

2 carrots, sliced

1 apple, cored and diced

1/2 cup basil leaves

1 tablespoon honey

3 cups cold water

Mint leafs (for garnish)

Place all the ingredients into a blender and blend until smooth. Pour into glass and garnish the top with a couple of fresh raspberries and a mint leaf if desired.

Super Powered Smoothie

This smoothie will boost your energy level with all its high in vitamins and minerals ingredients such as avocado, spinach, carrots and more.

2 carrots, sliced

1/4 cup raw baby spinach

1/4 cup chopped avocado

3 tablespoons wheatgrass juice

1 tablespoon ground flaxseed

1 tablespoon fresh ginger

1/4 cup crushed ice

2 tablespoons fresh cilantro, chopped

2 tablespoons fresh lemon juice

1/8 teaspoon sea salt

Place all the ingredients into a blender and blend until smooth. Pour into a chilled glass and garnish with a slice of lemon on the rim.

Grape Apple Smoothie

The awesome heart healthy apple has only 95 calories, 4 grams of fiber, antioxidant compounds plus aids in weight loss. Go Apple!!

1 apple, cored & diced

1 cup seedless grapes

1 carrot, diced

2 cups baby spinach

1/2 cup cold water or coconut water

Mint leafs (for garnish)

Place all the ingredients into a blender and blend until smooth. Pour into glass and garnish top with one or two mint leaves if desired.

Delicious Pear Smoothie

Pears do the body good with antioxidants like vitamins C & K plus copper, all of which protect cells from damaging free radicals.

4 pears, cored & chopped

2 cups almond milk

1/4 cup raw almonds

2 cups spinach, loosely packed

1 tablespoon honey, optional

Place all the ingredients into a blender and blend until smooth. Pour into glass and place a few slivered almonds on top.

Very Berry Kale Smoothie

Kale is probably the healthiest among all the greens as it is high in fiber, calcium, vitamins A, C & K and a great detox food. Start drinking!

1/2 cup frozen strawberries

1/2 cup frozen cherries or blueberries

1/2 cup pear nectar

1/8 teaspoon ground cinnamon

2 large leafs of kale

2 teaspoons flax seed oil (optional)

1 1/2 tablespoons Greek yogurt

Place all the ingredients into a blender and blend until smooth. Pour into glass and place a strawberry on the rim for added visual appeal.

Cantaloupe Smoothie

This wonderful melon has beta-carotene for healthy lungs, immune system booster vitamin C and potassium which reduces stress.

2 cups cantaloupe, peeled & diced

1 cup Greek yogurt, plain

1 tablespoon honey

3 tablespoons gelatin

2 cups crushed ice

Mint leafs (for garnish)

Place all the ingredients into a blender and blend until smooth. Pour into glass and garnish top with a mint leaf if desired.

Zucchini Summer Smoothie

Zucchini is chunk full of healthy ingredients such as potassium, magnesium, dietary fiber, vitamins A & C, and manganese. You go Zucchini!

1 cup zucchini, diced

1 orange, peeled & de-seeded

1/2 cup frozen berries

1 cup spinach or kale

1/2 cup Greek yogurt

1 tablespoon chia seeds

1 tablespoon flax seeds

1/2 tablespoon honey

Place all the ingredients into a blender and blend until smooth. Pour into a chilled glass and place a sliced of zucchini on the rim.

The Tomato Smoothie

The tasty tomato has beta-carotene which protects our skin from sun damage and lycopene that helps keep unwanted wrinkles at bay.

6 medium sized tomatoes, quartered

4 medium sized carrots, diced

1 large stick of celery, diced

1 teaspoon black pepper

2 tablespoons lemon juice

1 cup crushed ice

Place all the ingredients into a blender and blend until smooth. Pour into glasses and add a stick of celery into smoothie for garnishment.

Delicious Date Smoothie

Dates are high in fiber which promotes a healthy colon, plus rich in magnesium, vitamin B6 and more. That's one good Date!

5 pitted dates

3 tablespoons almond butter

1 cup plain yogurt

1 cup apple juice

1 cup crushed ice

Place all the ingredients into a blender and blend until smooth. Pour into glass and sprinkle chopped almonds on top.

Ginger & Banana Smoothie

Ginger loves your tummy by relieving indigestion, heartburn, nausea and other stomach disorders.

1/2 teaspoon fresh ginger, grated

1 ripe banana, sliced

1 tablespoon honey

3/4 cup plain or vanilla yogurt

Place all the ingredients into a blender and blend until smooth. Pour into glasse and place a single slice of banana on the rim.

Dreamy Orange Smoothie

Oranges are chunk full of vitamin C which helps keep the immune system working like a champ.

2 1/2 tablespoons orange juice concentrate

1/4 cup plain yogurt

1 navel orange, peeled

1/4 teaspoon vanilla or almond extract

4 to 5 ice cubes

Place all the ingredients into a blender and blend until smooth. Pour into glass and place a sprinkle of grated orange peel on top.

Berry, Banana & Soy Smoothie

From relieving postmenopausal symptoms to accelerating calcium absorption to our bones, soy milk can be a girl's best friend.

1 1/4 cups soy milk

1/2 frozen banana, sliced

1/2 cup frozen blueberries

2 teaspoons of sugar

1 teaspoon vanilla extract

Place all the ingredients into a blender and blend until smooth. Pour into glass and sprinkle the top with diced banana.

Apricot & Mango Smoothie

The eyes have it good when consuming the tasty apricot, which is known to be beneficial in aiding in the cure of macular degeneration, strengthening optic nerves and more.

2 cups apricots, diced (peel if desired)

2 cups mangos, peeled & diced

1 cup plain yogurt

4 teaspoons fresh lemon juice

1/4 teaspoon vanilla or almond extract

7 ice cubes

Place all the ingredients into a blender and blend until smooth. Pour into glass and top with a lemon twist for garnish.

Radish & Fruit Smoothie

Radishes are chunk full of health benefits such as vitamin C, B-complex, phosphorus, aids in respiratory and digestive health, plus so much more.

2 cups frozen strawberries

1 1/2 cups fresh watermelon, remove seeds

1 cup fresh cantaloupe

1 ripe banana

4 or 5 large red radishes

1 cup coconut water with pulp

Place all the ingredients into a blender and blend until smooth. Pour into glass and place diced watermelon on top for added appeal.

Blackberry Smoothie

Blackberries are high in antioxidants, calcium, zinc, vitamins B5, C, E, K plus folate.

1 1/2 cups blackberries

1 cup red watermelon, diced

1 ripe banana

2 cups kale or baby spinach

1/4 cup water (optional)

Place all the ingredients into a blender and blend until smooth. Pour into glass and place a single blackberry on top for garnish.

Acai & Cherry Smoothie

The mighty Acai berry rates high in antioxidants which is good for the heart, skin, digestive system, weight loss and more.

1 cup fresh acai berry

1 cup frozen cherries

2 small ripe bananas

4 ounces filtered water

Place all the ingredients into a blender and blend until smooth. Pour into glass and place a slice of banana on the rim.

Sweet Potato Smoothie

A cooked sweet potato is high in vitamins B6, C and D, plus iron and the anti-stress mineral magnesium.

1/2 cup cooked then cooled sweet potato

1 ripe banana

2 cups raw baby spinach

1/8 teaspoon all-spice

4 ounces coconut or hazelnut milk

Cinnamon (for garnish)

Place all the ingredients into a blender and blend until smooth. Pour into glass and sprinkle a little cinnamon on top.

Peachy Coconut Smoothie

The delicious coconut is heart healthy, high in dietary fiber, boosts the metabolism, and improves digestion plus so much more. Go Coconuts!

Meat from one coconut

1 cup coconut water

1 large peach, diced

2 cups kale or baby spinach

Place all the ingredients into a blender and blend until smooth. Pour into glass and sprinkle a little shredded coconut on top for added appeal.

Peanut Butter & Banana Smoothie

The health benefits of energy boosting peanut butter include, protein, fiber, potassium, unsaturated fats and tastes good too.

2 small ripe bananas

1 tablespoon peanut butter, heaping

1 tablespoon cacao powder

3 cups fresh baby spinach

8 ounces hazelnut milk

Place all the ingredients into a blender and blend until smooth. Pour into glass and place a slice of banana on the rim for garnish.

Simple Pear Smoothie

A single pear contains 3.1 grams of dietary fiber which aids in eliminating harmful toxins that can cause cancer and other ailments.

1 pear, cored

5 strawberries

1 cup kale or spinach

1 cup soy or almond milk

1 cup ice

Place all the ingredients into a blender and blend until smooth. Pour into glass and sprinkle the top with a diced strawberry.

Plum Smoothie

The high in fiber plum contains sorbitol and isatin which helps keep your digestive system running smooth.

3 to 4 plums, medium size (remove seed)

1 cup almond milk

1/2 cup plain yogurt

1 teaspoon honey, optional

Cinnamon (for garnish)

Place all the ingredients into a blender and blend until smooth. Pour into glass and sprinkle top with cinnamon.

Kick Start Grapefruit Smoothie

The eyes have it!! Grapefruit contains carotenoids that our bodies convert into vitamin A which is beneficial to our eyes and skin; great for breakfast or anytime.

4 grapefruit sections, seeded

1/2 cup granola

1 ripe banana

1/2 cup almond or soy milk

1/2 cup plain yogurt

Add ice if desired

Place all the ingredients into a blender and blend until smooth. Pour into glass then top with a little diced banana.

Lime & Lemon Detox Smoothie

Enjoy this delicious and refreshing smoothie that will aid in ridding your body of built-up toxins.

1 lime, peeled and seeded

1 lemon, peeled and seeded

1 cup coconut water or filtered water

1 ripe banana, frozen if desired

1 cup kale, remove stems

1 teaspoon honey

1/8 teaspoon sea salt

Place all the ingredients into a blender and blend until smooth. Pour into glass and drink up!

Rolled Oats Smoothie

Here is a breakfast smoothie that is both healthy and satisfying to help get your day off to a good start.

1/2 cup rolled oats

1 ripe banana

12 strawberries, frozen

1 1/2 teaspoons sugar (optional)

1 cup soy or almond milk

1/2 teaspoon vanilla

Place all the ingredients into a blender and blend until smooth. Pour into glass then top with a diced strawberry if desired.

Dark Chocolate Smoothie

Delicious dark chocolate contains fiber, cooper, magnesium, iron, manganese and more.

2 frozen bananas

1 1/2 cups almond milk

1 teaspoon unsweetened dark cocoa powder

2 tablespoons flax seed meal

2 tablespoons peanut butter

2 tablespoons dark chocolate chips

Place all the ingredients into a blender and blend until smooth. Pour into glass then top with a few chocolate chips for garnishment.

Almond and Apple Smoothie

The mighty almond is chunk full of protein, vitamins, minerals and fiber. Apparently dynamite does come in small packages!

1 medium apple, cored

1 tablespoon almond butter

1/2 ripe banana

3/4 cup almond milk, sweet or un-sweet

2 ice cubes

1/4 teaspoon ground cinnamon

Place all ingredients into a blender and blend until smooth. Pour into glass and top with a diced banana and a sprinkle of cinnamon. So good!

Christmas Smoothie

This creamy holiday smoothie not only tastes great but is also full of healthy ingredients such as bananas and dates.

1 ripe banana, frozen

3 cups almond milk, sweet or un-sweet

1/2 teaspoon almond extract

1/2 teaspoon cinnamon

2 or 3 pitted dates

1/2 teaspoon nutmeg

Mini candy canes (for garnish)

Place all ingredients into a blender and blend until smooth. Pour into glass and top with a sprinkle of nutmeg and a small candy cane on the rim.

Sweet Macadamia Smoothie

Straight from the rain forest, the macadamia nut will enrich your diet with fiber, calcium, selenium, zinc and magnesium.

1 ripe banana, frozen

1 cup coconut water

10 macadamia nuts

2 tablespoons cocoa powder

1 date, pitted

2 tablespoons sugar or coconut sugar

1/8 teaspoon salt

5 or 6 ice cubes

Place all ingredients into a blender and blend until smooth. Pour into glass and top with shredded coconut and chopped macadamias.

Energy Booster Smoothie

Here is a smoothie that will help boost your health and energy any time of day; just start blending.

1 cup kale

1 ripe banana

1 1/2 cups coconut milk

1 tablespoon honey

1 tablespoon flaxseed, ground

1/4 teaspoon coconut extract

3 or 4 ice cubes

Place all ingredients into a blender and blend until smooth. Pour into glass and top with diced banana and shredded coconut if desired.

Brazil Smoothie

Brazil nuts do the body good by providing selenium, vitamin E, lowering LDL, gluten free and so much more.

3 Brazil nuts, chopped

1 cup blueberries, frozen or fresh

1/2 cup strawberries, frozen or fresh

1 tablespoon flaxseed, ground

1 tablespoon sunflower seeds

Place all ingredients into a blender and blend until smooth. Pour into glass and place a sliced strawberry on the rim.

Fruity Tofu Smoothie

Tofu is a plant based food that is low in calories, gluten free and provides the body with iron, calcium and protein. Get your Tofu here.

1 ripe banana

6 ounces Tofu

2/3 cup soy milk

1 cup blueberries, frozen or fresh

1 tablespoon honey

3 ice cubes

Place all ingredients into a blender and blend until smooth. Pour into glass and place a 2 or 3 blueberries on top

Dragon Fruit Smoothie

The exotic dragon fruit boost the immunity system, delays the aging of skin cells, helps manage blood sugar levels and more.

1/2 dragon fruit

1/2 cup mixed berries, frozen

1 1/2 cups soy milk

1 tablespoon chia seeds

1 teaspoon honey, (optional)

Place all ingredients into a blender and blend until smooth. Pour into glass and place a berry on top.

Kid's Smoothie Pop

This frozen smoothie pop has healthy yogurt and fruit but your kids will only know it tastes good and is fun to eat.

1/2 cup whole milk

1/2 cup Greek yogurt, plain or vanilla

1 cup blueberries or other berries, frozen

Place ingredients into blender and blend until smooth. Pour into five 3 oz. paper cups, place in freezer until almost frozen then insert popsicle sticks, put back into freezer until completely frozen, tear off paper cup and serve.

Hazelnut and Chocolate Smoothie

Hazelnuts are rich in Vitamin E which helps protect the skin from harmful ultraviolet rays plus these little nuts contain magnesium for regulating calcium and more.

1 ripe banana

1 teaspoon honey

1 cup soy milk

2 teaspoons hazelnuts, chopped

1/2 teaspoon nutmeg

Place all ingredients into a blender and blend until smooth. Pour into glass and sprinkle the top with chopped hazelnuts and bananas.

Peachy Spinach Smoothie

This is a delicious smoothie that will give you all the health benefits of spinach and peaches all in one smoothie.

1 1/2 cups baby spinach

2 cups sliced peaches, frozen

1 teaspoon ginger root, thinly sliced

2 teaspoons honey

1 1/4 cups coconut or filtered water

Place all ingredients into a blender and blend until smooth. Pour into glass and place a single peach slice on top for garnish.

grab & go granola

GRANOLA
Homemade Granola

3 cups rolled oats (not instant)
1/2 teaspoon ground cinnamon
3 tablespoons light brown sugar, packed
1/4 teaspoon kosher salt
1/4 cup vegetable oil
1 teaspoon vanilla
1/3 cup honey
1/2 cup dried fruit, finely diced
1/2 cup walnuts, coarsely chopped

Preheat oven to 300 degrees F.

In a large bowl combine oats, cinnamon, brown sugar and kosher salt. In a separate small bowl mix together the oil, vanilla and honey. Pour the honey mixture over the oat mixture and mix until the oats are completely coated. On a rimmed baking sheet spread the mixture into a thin and even layer.

Bake in preheated oven on center rack for 15 minutes. Remove and stir, then return to oven and bake until the granola is a light golden brown, approximately 5 to 15 minutes.

Let the baking sheet cool on a wire rack to room temperature, stir occasionally, about 20 minutes. (Granola will harden as it cools down.) Add the dried fruit and walnuts to the mixture then toss to combine.

Store granola in one or more air-tight containers.

Awesome Applesauce Granola

1/2 cup toasted pecans, chopped

3 1/2 cups old-fashioned oats

1/4 cup ground flaxseed meal

1 tablespoon canola oil

1 tablespoon honey

1/2 cup applesauce, unsweetened

2 teaspoons cinnamon

1/4 teaspoon salt

1/2 cup coconut, flaked or shredded

1/2 cup dried cherries or cranberries (optional)

Preheat oven to 275 degrees F.

Place the pecans, oats and ground flax in a medium sized bowl and mix together. Combine the canola oil, honey, applesauce, cinnamon and salt in a small microwave save bowl. Microwave on high for 1 minute, stir mixture after 30 seconds, then return to microwave for another 30 seconds.

Pour the heated honey mixture over the oat mixture and mix well, then mix in the coconut. Spread granola on a baking sheet lined with parchment paper. Bake for 1 hour in preheated oven, stirring every 10 to 15 minutes. Remove from oven and let cool completely. Stir in dried fruit, if desired.

Store granola in one or more air-tight containers.

Nuts & Coconut Granola

1 cup almonds, slivered

1 cup cashews, halved

3 cups rolled oats

1/4 cup dark brown sugar

3/4 cup sweet coconut, shredded

1/4 cup vegetable oil

1/4 cup maple syrup

3/4 teaspoon salt

1 cup raisins

Preheat oven to 250 degrees F.

Combine the nuts, oats, brown sugar and coconut in a large bowl. In another bowl, mix together the oil, syrup, and salt. Combine both the mixtures and spread out evenly onto two sheet pans. Cook in preheated oven for 1 hour and 15 minutes, stir mixture every 15 minutes.

Remove from oven, let cool and pour into a large bowl, then stir in the raisins.

Store granola in one or more air-tight containers.

Chunky Chow Granola

1/3 cup brown sugar, packed
4 teaspoons vanilla
1/3 cup maple syrup
1/2 cup vegetable oil
1 or 1/2 teaspoon sea salt
5 cups old-fashioned rolled oats
1/2 cup pecans, chopped
1/2 cup walnuts, chopped
1 cup almonds, chopped
1/2 cup dates, chopped
1/2 cup dried cranberries
1/2 cup dried blueberries
1/2 cup white raisins, chopped
Preheat oven to 325 degrees F.

Whisk together the brown sugar, vanilla, maple syrup, oil, and sea salt in a large bowl. Add the nuts and oats into the brown sugar mixture and blend well. Place the mixture onto a baking sheet lined with parchment paper. Press the granola mixture down with a spatula to form a compact single layer.

Bake on middle rack in preheated oven for 30 - 35 minutes, then rotate pan once after fifteen minutes. Remove from oven and let cool for approximately an hour. Break-up the cooled granola into pieces. Mix in the dates, dried cranberries, blueberries, raisins and shredded sweet coconut.

Store granola in one or more air-tight containers.

Crunchy Cranberry Granola

1/4 cup honey

1/2 cup canola oil (use less for a crunchier granola)

1 cup almonds, sliced

6 cups whole oats

2 teaspoons cinnamon

1/2 cup dried cranberries

Preheat oven to 350 degrees F.

Place honey and canola oil in a microwave save bowl and mix together, then microwave on high for one minute. In a medium sized bowl mix together the remainder of the ingredients (except the dried cranberries).

Line a baking sheet with parchment paper and spread out the dry mixture. Pour heated oil and honey onto dry granola and toss until well coated. Bake in preheated oven for 20 minutes; stir half way through cooking time. Let granola cool then stir in the dried cranberries.

Store granola in one or more air-tight containers.

HEALTHY IN A HURRY: SMOOTHIE RECIPES, BARS AND GRAB & GO SNACKS

BARS & COOKIES

Chewy Date and Cranberry Bars

1 cup dates
1/4 cup honey
1/4 cup peanut butter, smooth or crunchy
1 cup unsalted peanuts or almonds, chopped
1 1/2 cups rolled oats
1/2 cup dried cranberries (optional)

Place dates into a food processor or blender and process for approximately 1 minute or until dates are the consistency of dough. Spread the oats out onto a shallow baking pan and toast in a preheated 350 degree F. oven for about 15 minutes or until lightly browned. Place dates, nuts, oats and cranberries into a bowl, then set aside. In a small saucepan warm the honey and peanut butter over low heat, stirring constantly. Pour honey mixture over the oat mixture and mix well.

Place mixture onto an 8 x 8 inch dish lined with parchment paper. Spread mixture out evenly while pressing it down into the pan. Cover top with plastic wrap and place in the refrigerator for 20 minutes. Remove from pan and cut into ten evenly sized bars.

Store bars in the refrigerator in one or more air tight containers.

Microwave Breakfast Squares

1/2 cup roasted sunflower seeds, shelled

2 cups instant oatmeal, uncooked

1/2 cup roasted peanuts

1/2 cup dried cranberries

2 cups Rice Krispies cereal

1/2 cup brown sugar, packed

1/2 cup light corn syrup

1/2 cup crunchy peanut butter

1 teaspoon vanilla

Place the first 5 ingredients into a large bowl and mix well (set aside). With an electric mixer on high speed mix together the brown sugar, light corn syrup and crunchy peanut butter in a medium sized microwave save bowl, once mixed blend in the vanilla. Pour the brown sugar mixture over the dry mixture and mix until well blended.

Once mixed pour into an 8 x 8 inch pan lined with parchment paper and press evenly into pan. Let cool for an hour or longer, cut into squares.

Store squares in one or more sealed containers.

No Bake Bars

1 cup crunchy peanut butter

3 cups rolled oats

1/2 cup honey

2 tablespoons (level) whey protein

Mix together crunchy peanut butter and honey in a large nonstick saucepan and warm over low heat until thin, stirring constantly. Mix in the rolled oats and whey protein powder.

Once mixed pour into a 9 x 9 inch pan lined with parchment paper and press evenly into pan. Cover cooled pan with plastic wrap and continue to let cool in refrigerator for 2 to 3 hours before cutting into bars.

Store bars in one or more sealed containers.

Makes 16 bars.

Peanut Butter Bars

For best results, let baked bars cool completely before cutting.

3 to 4 cups rolled oats

2 tablespoons shelled sun flower seeds or chia seeds

1/2 cup pecans, chopped

3/4 cup smooth or crunchy peanut butter, melted

1/2 cup honey

1/2 cup dried cherries or chocolate chips

Preheat oven to 350 degrees F.

In a large mixing bowl, mix together rolled oats, chia seeds and pecans. Add honey and mix well. Add the melted peanut butter and mix until completely moistened. Easily fold the cherries or chocolate chips into dough. If the dough seems to dry add a tablespoon of honey or melted peanut butter until moist.

Press dough in a 9 x 13 baking dish that has been lined with parchment paper. Bake in preheated oven for 25 minutes. Let cool completely before cutting.

Store bars in one or more sealed containers.

Makes 12-16 bars

Almond Coconut Bars

1/2 cup shredded coconut

1/3 cup almonds, slivered

11 dates, pitted

1/4 cup cashews

1 teaspoon coconut oil

Blend together the coconut and almonds in a food processor; add the dates and pulse until well combined. Add the coconut oil and cashews; pulse until the mixture is thickened and clings together.

Place mixture onto a sheet of parchment paper; shape into a single square, folding sides of parchment paper over the top. Place in refrigerator for 30 minutes or longer then cut into bars.

Store bars in one or more sealed containers.

Marvelous Molasses Bars

1/4 cup maple syrup
1 cup dates, pitted
1/3 cup molasses
3/4 teaspoon vanilla
1/8 teaspoon cloves
1/4 teaspoon nutmeg
1 teaspoon cinnamon
1 1/2 teaspoons ginger, ground
1/4 teaspoon salt
2 1/2 cups old-fashioned rolled oats
1/2 cup dried apricots
1/2 cup dried cherries or cranberries
2/3 cup pecans, chopped
1/3 cup sunflower seeds, shelled & unsalted

Preheat oven to 325 degrees F.

Place the maple syrup, dates, molasses and vanilla in a food processor and pulse 3 times. To this add the cloves, nutmeg, cinnamon, ginger and salt; puree until smooth. Add the rolled oats and pulse until coarsely chopped. Remove mixture from processor and place in a medium size bowl making sure all of the mixture is removed. Mix in the apricots, cherries, pecans and sunflower seeds.

Once mixed pour into an 8 x 8 inch pan lined with parchment paper and press evenly into pan. Bake in preheated oven for 25 minutes. Once done let cool then place in the freezer until bars are set. Cut into 8 to 12 bars.

Store bars in one or more sealed containers.

Makes 8 to 12 bars.

Cinnamon Granola Bars

Use a sheet of parchment paper or a greased spatula when pressing bar mixture into a prepared dish.

3/4 cup brown sugar, packed
1/2 cup applesauce
1 egg
2 tablespoons honey
2 tablespoons ground flaxseed
1 cup white wheat flour
1 teaspoon cinnamon
2 cups old-fashioned/rolled oats
1/2 teaspoon baking soda
1/2 cup white raisins

Preheat oven to 350 degrees F.

In a large mixing bowl, beat brown sugar and applesauce until it becomes crumbly. Add egg and beat well. Stir in honey and ground flaxseed. In a small bowl, combine the flour, cinnamon, oats and baking soda; mix into sugar mixture until just blended. Slowly stir in the white raisins.

Press into an 11 x 7 inch. baking dish lined with parchment paper. Bake in preheated oven for 14 to 18 minutes or until the edges are lightly brown. Cool completely on a wire rack and then cut into bars.

Store bars in one or more sealed containers.

Gluten Free Bars

1/2 cup honey

1 cup coconut oil

1 teaspoon vanilla

1/2 teaspoon sea salt

1/2 cup gluten-free all purpose flour

1/2 cup brown rice flour

4 cups gluten-free oats

1/2 cup chocolate chips

Preheat oven to 350 degrees F.

In a large mixing bowl stir together honey and coconut oil. Add vanilla, salt, flour and rice flour and mix well. Add the oats one cup at a time to mixture and stir until completely mixed, then gently stir in chocolate chips. Add nuts if desired.

Press the mixture evenly into an 11 x 7 inch baking dish lined with parchment paper. Bake in preheated oven for approximately 25 minutes, let cool completely before cutting.

Store bars in one or more sealed containers.

Granola Energy Balls

2 cups shredded coconut

2 cups oats

2/3 cup honey

2 teaspoons vanilla

1 teaspoon cinnamon

1 cup ground flaxseed

1 cup peanut butter

1 cup chocolate chips

Place all the ingredients into a large bowl and mix well. Wash hands thoroughly, then using the palm of your hands roll the batter into bite-size balls. (The size you make the balls will determine your yield).

Store balls in the refrigerator in one or more air tight containers.

Easy Pumpkin Seed Bars

1 cup puffed millet

2 cups oats

1/4 cup roasted pumpkin seeds

1/4 cup brown sugar, packed

1/4 cup honey

1/4 cup coconut oil

1 teaspoon vanilla

In a large bowl mix together the millet, oats and pumpkin seeds. Place sugar, honey and coconut oil into a small saucepan and stir together over medium heat until bubbly (approximately 2 minutes); stir constantly. Let the honey mixture cool for 2 or 3 minutes, then add the vanilla extract and mix well.

Pour the honey mixture over the oat mixture, and mix thoroughly. Line an 8 x 8 inch glass pan with parchment paper; then pour the mixture into the pan. Be sure to press down on the granola mixture firmly and evenly.

Place into the freezer for several minutes until set. Once mixture has set, turn the pan upside down onto a cutting board. Then cut into the size bars you like.

Store bars in one or more sealed containers.

Awesome Apricot Bars

Coat your knife with a little oil or butter to prevent sticking before cutting bars.

1 cup toasted pecans, chopped

1/4 cup peanut butter

1 large banana, mashed

1 teaspoon cinnamon

2/3 cup maple syrup

2 1/2 cups rolled oats (do not use instant)

1/3 cup white raisins

1/3 cup apricots, chopped

Preheat oven to 325 degrees F.

Place chopped pecans in a single layer on a baking sheet and toast in preheated oven for 10 or 12 minutes. Place the peanut butter and banana into a large mixing bowl and stir together until well mixed. Add the ground cinnamon and syrup then whisk until combined. Mix in the rolled oats adding more peanut butter or syrup if required.

Stir the toasted pecans into the batter then add the white raisins and apricots. Line an 8 X 8 inch pan with parchment paper and pour batter onto pan. Press the mixture down into pan firmly and evenly. Bake in preheated oven for 25 minutes then remove from oven and let cool for approximately 1 hour before cutting into bars or squares.

Store bars in one or more sealed containers.

Kid's Favorite Breakfast Bars

1 cup pecans, chopped
1 cup rolled oats
1 cup wheat flake cereal
1/2 cup honey
1 cup dried cranberries
1/8 teaspoon salt

Spread the chopped pecans, oats and wheat flakes on a baking sheet. Place in oven and bake in preheated oven at 400 degrees F., until starting to brown, approximately ten minutes.

Pour the honey into a large saucepan and heat over medium/high setting, without stirring, until large bubbles form and it starts to darken on the outer edges, about 2 to 4 minutes. (The bubbles will increase to about 3/4 inch or larger when the honey is done.)

Pour the toasted pecan mixture into the heated honey, add the dried cranberries and salt and stir until completely coated. Spray a 9 inch glass pie pan with non-stick spray. Pour the granola into the pie pan.

Press mixture down firmly and evenly into pan using a heat-resistant spatula that is coated with non-stick spray. Let cool for 30 minutes to 1 hour. Once bars have cooled cut into wedges and place on a wire rack to cool completely before serving.

Store bars in one or more sealed containers.

Nutty Energy Bar

1/2 cup pecans, raw

1/2 cup walnuts, raw

1 cup almonds, raw

12 medium sized dates

Blend the pecans, walnuts and almonds in a food processor until they have a fine consistency. Mix in the dates. (The nuts have natural oils so there is no need for water.)

Line an 8 x 8 inch pan with parchment paper; make sure the parchment paper runs up the sides. Lay an extra piece of parchment paper on top of dough and press down firmly and evenly into the pan. Place in the refrigerator to set about two hours. Once chilled, cut into squares.

Store bars in one or more sealed containers.

Chocolate and Peanut Bar

To keep bars or squares from sticking together, place parchment paper between them.

2 cups peanuts, raw

1/8 teaspoon sea salt

12 pitted dates, medium size

3 tablespoons water (if needed)

1/4 cup chocolate chips

Place the peanuts, sea salt and dates into a food processor or blender and blend into a powder. If moisture is needed, slowly add a little water until a dough is formed.

Line an 8 x 8 inch glass baking dish with parchment paper and leave room for some paper to stick out from the sides. Slowly spoon the dough evenly into the glass dish. (The dough will be sticky; therefore you may want to wet or butter your spoon.) Pack the dough down with the extended parchment paper until flat and even.

Sprinkle chocolate chips on top and press into dough. Place in the refrigerator until set.

Store bars in one or more sealed containers.

Chewy Fruity & Nutty Bars

1 teaspoon plus 2 tablespoons unsalted butter
1 cup dried cranberries
1/2 cup dried apricots, chopped
1 1/2 cups puffed brown rice cereal
1 cup almonds, whole
1/2 cup cashews, whole
1/4 cup unsalted almond butter, creamy
2 tablespoons brown sugar, firmly packed
1/4 teaspoon sea salt or table salt
1/2 cup brown rice syrup

Place cranberries, apricots, brown rice cereal, almonds, and cashews, into a large mixing bowl toss together then set aside.

Place the almond butter, brown sugar, 2 tablespoons butter, salt and syrup, into a small to medium size saucepan over medium heat. Bring to a simmer and cook for 1 minute, **stirring constantly** to prevent scorching. Pour over the cereal mixture in bowl. Mix together using a wooden spoon until well blended.

Line an 8 x 8 inch glass dish with aluminum foil, leaving an inch of overhang on the two opposite edges to use as a handle for later. Grease the foil with 1 teaspoon of melted butter. Press the mixture firmly and evenly onto the prepared dish using a sheet of parchment paper. Refrigerate for at least 1 hour.

Transfer from dish to a cutting board. Using a sharp buttered knife cut into 20 bars; then remove from foil. Store bars in the refrigerator inside an air-tight container, with sheets of parchment paper between layers. Makes 20 bars.

Poppin Popcorn Bars

1 cup dry-roasted peanuts, unsalted
1 1/2 cups regular oats
12 cups air-popped popcorn
5 tablespoons honey
1 cup applesauce
1 cup light brown sugar
1/4 teaspoon vanilla
1/2 teaspoon sea salt or kosher salt
1 1/2 cups white raisins
Preheat oven to 350 degrees F.

Spread out the roasted peanuts and oats on a baking sheet and bake for 12 minutes. Remove from the oven and let cool completely. Pour the popcorn into a very large glass bowl that has been sprayed with non-stick cooking spray.

Combine, honey, applesauce, and brown sugar in a medium size saucepan and heat over a medium heat stirring until mixture comes to a boil, then continue boiling for 1.5 minutes (stir constantly). Remove saucepan from heat and mix in vanilla and salt.

Pour the hot sugar mixture over the popcorn and mix together until popcorn is well coated. Mix in the reserved oats and peanut mixture and raisins. Spread evenly in a 13 x 9 inch baking pan lined with parchment paper or sprayed with non-stick baking spray.

Let cool in refrigerator for approximately 30 minutes or longer if needed. Once cooled turn-out onto a large cutting board, cut into 24 equal bars.

Store bars in one or more sealed containers.

Makes 24 bars.

Healthy Banana Nut Cookies

1/4 cup coconut oil, melted
1 teaspoon vanilla
3 ripened bananas, mashed
1/4 cup pure maple syrup
2/3 cup almond meal
1/4 cup wheat germ
1 cup old fashioned oats
1/2 cup walnuts, chopped
1/2 teaspoon baking powder
1/2 cup shredded coconut, unsweetened

Preheat oven to 350 degrees F.

In a large mixing bowl combine the coconut oil, vanilla, mashed banana and maple syrup. In another bowl, mix together the almond meal, wheat germ, oats, walnuts, baking powder, and coconut. Add dry ingredients to the banana mixture and mix well.

Line 2 cookie sheets with parchment paper then drop extra large spoonfuls of batter onto prepared cookie sheets. Bake for 16-18 minutes until tops are golden brown.

Store cookies in one or more air-tight containers.

Morning Cookies

1/2 cup pecans, chopped
1 package refrigerated oatmeal raisin cookies, Big Deluxe
1/2 cup flaked coconut
1 cup carrots, finely shredded
1 tablespoon grated orange peel
2 1/2 cups wheat flake cereal, crushed to 1 cup
1/2 teaspoon salt
3/4 teaspoon cinnamon
3 orange slices, optional
3 large strawberries, optional

Glaze:

1 1/2 cups powdered sugar
2 tablespoons fresh orange juice

Preheat oven to 350 degrees F.

Spread pecans out on a 15x10 inch sheet pan with sides. Place in preheated oven and bake for 6 to 10 minutes, stirring occasionally, until toasted. In a large bowl, tear up the Big Deluxe cookie dough into smaller pieces. Add toasted pecans, coconut, carrots, orange peel, cereal, salt, and cinnamon. Mix with wooden spoon until well combined.

Divide dough into twelve equal portions. Line two cookie sheets with parchment paper. Put six portions on each cookie sheet. Flatten each portion to approximately 2 3/4 inch round.

Bake for 14 to 17 minutes or until golden brown. Once done let cool on cookie sheets for 3 minutes. Place cookies on cooling racks and cool completely for about 15 minutes.

Glaze: Place orange juice and powdered sugar in a small bowl and blend well. Drizzle orange glaze over cookies.

Place glazed cookies on serving platter and garnish with orange slices and strawberries.

Store cookies in one or more air-tight containers.

Easy Oatmeal Banana Cookies

1/2 medium ripened banana, mashed
1 egg white
1 tablespoon almond or soy milk
1/4 cup + 1 tablespoon rolled oats
1 teaspoon cinnamon
1 teaspoon vanilla
2 tablespoons maple syrup
1/4 teaspoon baking powder
1/2 cup walnuts, chopped

Place the mashed banana into a medium size bowl and whisk in the egg whites. Add the remainder of the ingredients and using a fork mix together well. Place mixture into the microwave for one minute and 30 to 45 seconds; let cool, spoon out portions on to a platter or plate and shape into a cookie. If desired serve with preserves, honey or your favorite jam.

Store cookies in one or more air-tight containers.

Super Charged Breakfast Cookies

3 3/4 cups old fashioned oats, divided
1/4 cup flaxseed, ground
1/2 teaspoon salt
1/2 teaspoon baking soda
1/4 cup + 2 tablespoons honey
1 medium ripened banana, mashed
1/4 cup + 1 tablespoon coconut oil, melted
1/2 cup applesauce, unsweetened
1 lemon, squeezed for juice and zest
1 tablespoon lemon zest
3 cups blackberries, fresh

Preheat oven to 350 degrees F.

Place 1 3/4 cups oats into a food processor then process for four minutes or until very fine in texture. In a large mixing bowl mix together the processed oats, remaining oats, ground flaxseed, salt and baking soda. To this add the honey, banana, coconut oil, applesauce, lemon juice and lemon zest, then mix together until just combined. Easily fold in the 3 cups of blackberries. Let batter sit for ten minutes to thicken.

Line a baking sheet with parchment paper. Scoop 1/4 cup batter onto prepared baking sheet then using the wet bottom of a glass press batter down slightly to flatten. Bake in preheated oven for 8 to 10 minutes. Cookies should be golden brown when done. Let cool completely.

Store cookies in one or more air-tight containers.

Nutty Morning Cookies

1/2 cup applesauce, unsweetened
1/4 cup honey
1/2 teaspoon table salt
1/2 teaspoon baking soda
2 cups whole wheat flour
1 teaspoon vanilla extract
1 cup dried cranberries
1 cup pecans, finely chopped

Glaze:

1 tablespoon cranberry juice, unsweetened
1/2 cup plus 2 tablespoons powdered sugar

Place applesauce, honey, and salt into a large mixing bowl and mix with an electric mixer at medium-low speed until creamy. Add the baking soda, wheat flour, and vanilla, and beat for one minute or until well blended. Blend in the dried cranberries and chopped pecans.

Shape cookie dough into a large log (approximately three inches in diameter); wrap in parchment paper. Place in the refrigerator and let chill 8 hours or up to one week. Slice the dough into 1/2 inch slices then place on a cookie sheet lined with parchment paper. Bake in a 325 degrees F. preheated oven for 20 minutes. Let cool. Mix together cranberry juice and powdered sugar. Drizzle glaze over cookies.

Store cookies in one or more air-tight containers.

Sunshine Pumpkin Cookies

1/2 cup almond butter, raw
1/4 cup honey, raw
1/2 teaspoon baking soda
2 teaspoons pumpkin pie spice
1/2 cup pureed pumpkin
2 eggs
1/2 teaspoon vanilla
1/4 teaspoon sea salt or table salt
1 cup coconut, shredded
1 cup walnuts, finely chopped

Preheat oven to 350 degrees F.

Place all the ingredients into a large bowl and mix well. Line a cookie sheet with parchment paper and drop dough onto sheet with a tablespoon. Press dropped dough down slightly with the wet bottom of a glass. Bake in preheated oven for 12 to 15 minutes or until golden brown.

Store cookies in one or more air-tight containers.

MUFFINS
Fiber Rich Muffins

2 cups quick cooking oats
2 cups unsweetened shredded wheat cereal, crushed
2 cups bran cereal
1 cup boiling water
4 cups buttermilk
4 eggs, beaten
2 cups applesauce, unsweetened
4 tablespoons canola oil
2 1/4 cups brown sugar, packed
5 teaspoons baking soda
5 cups all-purpose flour
1 teaspoon salt
4 dozen muffin liners

Preheat oven to 400 degrees F.

Place oats, bran and wheat cereal into a large bowl and combine. Add water, buttermilk, eggs, applesauce and oil then stir for one minute. Mix in the brown sugar. In a separate bowl combine the baking soda, flour, and salt; then add to cereal mixture and blend well. Fill paper-lined muffin cups 3/4 full.

Bake in preheated oven for 18-20 minutes. Let cool for 10 minutes; remove muffins from pans onto wire racks.

Makes 4 dozen muffins.

Good Morning Muffins

1 cup sugar
2 cups whole wheat flour
2 teaspoons cinnamon
2 teaspoons baking soda
1/3 cup dried apricots, chopped
1/3 cup sunflower kernels
1/3 cup shredded coconut
2 cups shredded carrots
1/3 cup semisweet chocolate chips
1 ripe banana, mashed
1 cup applesauce, unsweetened
2 tablespoons canola oil
3 eggs
2 teaspoons vanilla extract
18 muffin liners

Preheat oven to 375 degrees F.

In a large mixing bowl combine sugar, wheat flour, cinnamon and baking soda. Add in the apricots, sunflower kernels, coconut, carrots and chocolate chips. Mix in the mashed banana. Beat together applesauce, oil, eggs and vanilla; stir into apricot mixture just until well moistened.

Fill each paper-lined muffin cup two thirds full. Bake in preheated oven for 18-22 minutes. Let cool for 5 minutes, and then remove from pans onto wire racks.

Makes 18 muffins.

Plenty Sweet Trail Mix

2 cups mini pretzels

2 cups multi-grain cheerios

1 cup dried cherries or cranberries

1/2 cup mixed nuts

1/2 cup dark chocolate semi-sweet morsels

1/2 cup white raisins

Mix together all the ingredients in a large mixing bowl.

Dried Cherry Muffins

1/3 cup sugar
4 1/2 teaspoons applesauce
2 tablespoons canola oil
1 medium egg
1/2 teaspoon baking soda
6 tablespoons all purpose flour
6 tablespoons whole wheat flour
1/4 teaspoon salt
1/4 cup buttermilk
1/4 cup dried cherries
Muffin liners

Preheat oven to 350 degrees F.

Cream together the sugar, applesauce and oil in a small mixing bowl, until fluffy and light. Beat in the egg. In a separate bowl mix together the baking soda, wheat flour, all purpose flour and salt; add this to the creamed mixture alternatively with the buttermilk. Beat mixture after each addition. Fold in the dried cherries.

With a tablespoon, spoon the batter into paper-lined muffin cups, filling 3/4 full with batter and bake in preheated oven for 20 to 25 minutes. Tops of muffins should spring back when touched lightly. Let cool on a wire rack.

Cinnamon & Apple Muffins

1 teaspoon baking soda
1 teaspoon cinnamon, ground
1 teaspoon nutmeg
1/4 cup flaxseed, ground
1 cup whole-wheat flour
1/2 cup oat-bran
1 1/2 teaspoon baking powder
4 tablespoons canola oil
1 egg, beaten
1/4 cup sugar
1/3 cup applesauce, unsweetened
1/4 cup chopped pecans
Muffin liners

Preheat oven to 350 degrees F.

Place the baking soda, cinnamon, nutmeg, flaxseed, wheat flour, oat bran and baking powder, into a large mixing bowl and whisk together. Using a separate mixing bowl whisk together canola oil and egg, blend well. Mix in the sugar and applesauce. Combine the two mixtures and fold-in the chopped pecans.

With a tablespoon, spoon the batter into paper-lined muffin cups, filling 3/4 full with batter and bake in preheated oven for 22 to 25 minutes. Tops of muffins should spring back when touched lightly. Let cool on a wire rack.

Pineapple & Papaya Muffins

1/2 teaspoon baking soda
2 teaspoons cinnamon
1 1/2 teaspoons baking powder
1 1/2 cups whole-wheat flour
1 cup papaya, cubed
1/3 cup plain yogurt
1/2 cup crushed pineapple, drained
1/4 cup sugar
1/4 cup agave syrup
2 tablespoons canola oil
1 medium egg, beaten
1/4 cup walnuts or pecans, chopped
1/2 cup cranberries, dried
12 muffin liners

Preheat oven to 375 degrees F.

Place baking soda, cinnamon, baking powder and whole-wheat flour into a large mixing bowl. Using a blender or a food processor puree the papaya, plain yogurt and pineapple. Add the sugar, agave syrup, oil and beaten egg then mix well. Combine for two mixtures and blend in the nuts and dried cranberries.

With a tablespoon, spoon batter into paper-lined muffin cups, filling 3/4 full with batter and bake in preheated oven 20 to 22 minutes. Tops of muffins should spring-back when touched lightly. Let cool on a wire rack.

Makes 12 muffins.

Yummy Pecan Pie Muffins

1 cup light brown sugar, packed
1/2 cup all-purpose flour
1/2 teaspoon baking powder
1 cup pecans, chopped
1/4 teaspoon salt
1 cup applesauce, unsweetened
2 tablespoon canola oil
2 large eggs, lightly beaten
1 teaspoon vanilla
1/2 cup pecans, finely chopped
Non-stick baking spray

Preheat oven to 425 degrees F.

Mix together the first five ingredients in a large glass bowl; in the center of the mixture make a well. Stir together the applesauce, oil, eggs and vanilla; add to the well of the dry mixture, and mix just until moistened.

Spray a 12 cup muffin pan with non-stick cooking spray. Put 1 teaspoon of the pecans (finely chopped) in each of the 12 muffin cups; spoon the batter over chopped pecans, filling each cup almost to top.

Bake in preheated oven for 10 to 12 minutes. Tops of muffins should spring-back when touched lightly. Run a knife around the edges of each muffin cup to loosen, and carefully remove from pans. Let cool on wire rack.

Makes 12 muffins.

Miniature Banana Muffins

1 teaspoon baking powder
1 teaspoon baking soda
1 1/2 cups all-purpose flour
1/2 teaspoon salt
3/4 cup white sugar
1 egg
3 large ripe bananas, mashed
2/3 cup applesauce, unsweetened
12 mini muffin liners
Preheat oven to 350 degrees F.

Into a mixing bowl sift together the baking powder, baking soda, flour and salt. In another bowl combine sugar, egg, bananas and applesauce. Blend in the dry mixture, and mix until completely smooth.

With a teaspoon, spoon batter into paper-lined muffin cups, filing 3/4 full with batter and bake in preheated oven for 10 to 15 minutes. Tops of muffins should spring-back when touched lightly. Let cool on wire rack.

Makes 12 muffins.

Christmas Cranberry Muffins

1 1/4 cups sugar
1 cup applesauce, unsweetened
2 tablespoons canola oil
2 eggs
1/2 cup 2 % milk
2 cups flour
2 teaspoons baking powder
1/4 teaspoon salt
2 cups frozen cranberries, coarsely chopped
1/2 cup chopped walnuts
12 muffin liners

Preheat oven to 350 degrees F.

In a medium sized mixing bowl mix together the sugar, applesauce and oil until well blended. Add one egg at a time, beating after each egg is added. Stir together baking powder, flour, and salt in a separate bowl. Add dry mixture alternately with the milk to the applesauce mixture. Mix in the cranberries and walnuts.

With a tablespoon, spoon batter into paper-lined muffin cups, filing 3/4 full with batter and bake in preheated oven for 25 to 30 minutes. Tops of muffins should spring-back when touched lightly. Let cool on wire rack.

Makes 12 muffins.

Easy Oatmeal Muffins

1 cup buttermilk
1 cup rolled oats
1/2 cup light brown sugar, packed
1 large egg, beaten lightly
1 cup applesauce, unsweetened
2 tablespoons canola oil
1 teaspoon baking powder
1 cup all-purpose flour
1/2 teaspoon baking soda
1/2 teaspoon salt
1/2 cup white raisins
12 muffin liners

Mix together buttermilk and oats in a large mixing bowl, set aside for one hour

Preheat oven to 400 degrees F.

Add brown sugar, egg, applesauce and oil to buttermilk mixture, stir together until just combined. Into another large bowl, sift together the baking powder, flour, baking soda and salt, then add to buttermilk mixture, stir together until just combined. Fold in the white raisins.

With a tablespoon, spoon batter into paper-lined muffin cups, filing 3/4 full with batter and bake in preheated oven for 20 to 25 minutes. Tops of muffins should spring-back when touched lightly. Let cool on wire rack.

Makes 12 muffins.

Nutty Coconut & Apple Muffins

1 1/2 teaspoons baking soda
1 1/2 cups flour
1/2 teaspoon nutmeg
3/4 teaspoon salt
1 cup + 2 tablespoons sugar
2 eggs
2/3 cup applesauce, unsweetened
1 1/2 cups walnuts, chopped
2 cups apples, peeled & diced
3/4 cup coconut, flaked
18 muffin liners

Preheat oven to 350 degrees F.

Place the baking soda, flour, nutmeg, and salt into a large bowl and combine. In a separate bowl beat the sugar and eggs, and then stir in applesauce, walnuts, apples, and coconut, mix in the dry ingredients. Stir until just moistened.

With a tablespoon, spoon batter into paper-lined muffin cups, filing 3/4 full with batter and bake in preheated oven for 25 to 30 minutes. Tops of muffins should spring-back when touched lightly. Let cool on wire rack.

Makes 18 muffins.

Carrot Muffins

1/2 teaspoon ginger
1 teaspoon cinnamon
1 teaspoon baking soda
1 1/2 cups whole wheat flour
1/2 teaspoon salt
1/2 cup honey
1 large egg
1 teaspoon vanilla
1/2 cup butter, softened
1 cup applesauce, unsweetened
3/4 cup carrot, grated

Preheat oven to 350 degrees F

Place ginger, cinnamon, baking soda, wheat flour and salt in a medium sized mixing bowl and whisk together. Using a electric mixer on medium speed mix together the honey, egg, vanilla and softened butter in a large bowl. Blend in the flour mixture on low speed until well mixed. Batter will be somewhat thick. Fold in the carrots and applesauce using a spatula.

With a tablespoon, spoon batter into paper-lined muffin cups, filing 3/4 full with batter and bake in preheated oven for 22 to 24 minutes. Tops of muffins should spring-back when touched lightly. Let cool on wire rack.

Makes 12 muffins.

Sweet Pumpkin Mini Muffins

2 cups flour
1 1/2 to 2 tablespoons pumpkin pie spice
1 teaspoon baking soda
2 eggs
1/2 cup brown sugar
1/2 cup sugar
1 ripe banana, mashed
3/4 cup pumpkin pie puree, canned
1/4 cup Greek yogurt, vanilla
1/2 cup applesauce, chunky style
36 mini muffin liners

Preheat oven to 350 degrees F.

Using a whisk sift together the flour, pumpkin pie spice and baking soda. Place eggs in separate bowl and using an electric mixer, beat until smooth, then add brown sugar and sugar and mix until smooth and light golden in color.

Place the mash banana into egg mixture, then spoon in pumpkin puree, Greek yogurt and applesauce and mix well on low to medium speed. Pour in flour mixture and continue mixing at low speed until fully combined.

With a tablespoon, spoon batter into paper-lined mini muffin cups, filling 3/4 full with batter and bake in preheated oven 13 to 17 minutes. Tops of muffins should spring-back when touched lightly. Let cool on a wire rack.

Makes 36 mini muffins.

HEALTHY IN A HURRY: SMOOTHIE RECIPES, BARS AND GRAB & GO SNACKS

trail mix and party mix

TRAIL MIX & PARTY MIX

Traveling Trail Mix

2 ounces crystallized ginger, sliced

1 1/2 cups almond or pecan granola cereal

1/2 cup hulled sunflower seeds

2 ounces dried mango, sliced

Place all of the above ingredients into a mixing bowl and stir together.

Store trail mix in one or more air-tight containers.

Super Crunchy Trail Mix

2 cups whole-grain Rice Chex

1/2 cup dried cherries

3 cups granola cereal

1/2 cup roasted pistachios, unsalted

Place all of the above ingredients into a mixing bowl and stir together.

Store trail mix in one or more air-tight containers.

Lunch Box Trail Mix

3/4 cup dried blueberries

2 cups animal crackers

2 1/2 cups air-popped popcorn

3/4 cup roasted pecan halves

Place all of the above ingredients into a mixing bowl and stir together.

Store trail mix in one or more air-tight containers.

Spiced Up Trail Mix

2 teaspoons ginger
1/4 cup brown sugar, firmly packed
2 teaspoons paprika
2 teaspoons cinnamon
1 cup rolled oats
1 cup whole almonds, raw
1 cup pistachios, shelled
1 cup pecan halves, raw
1 cup roasted and salted pumpkin seeds, shelled
1/4 cup apple juice concentrate, thawed
2/3 cup dried cherries or cranberries
2/3 cup white or golden raisins

Preheat oven to 250 degrees.

In a small bowl mix together the ginger, brown sugar, paprika and cinnamon then set aside. Place oats, almonds, pistachios, pecans and pumpkin seeds in large bowl. Add the apple juice concentrate and toss together until the nuts are well coated. Sprinkle on the brown sugar mixture, tossing until well coated.

Spread mixture out evenly on two 15 x 10 x 1 inch baking pans. Bake for 30 minutes in preheated oven, stir mixture after 15 minutes then return to oven. Let cool completely on a wire rack. Stir in raisins and cherries.

Store trail mix in one or more air-tight containers.

So-Good Party Mix

1 cup pumpkin seeds, raw
1/4 cup sesame seeds, raw
2 cups Bran Chex
2 cups Multigrain Cheerios
2 cups puffed rice cereal
1 tablespoon Worcestershire sauce
1 tablespoon sesame oil
1/2 teaspoon chili powder
1/2 cup canola oil
1/4 cup soy sauce
1/4 teaspoon sea salt or table salt

Preheat oven to 300 degrees F.

Place the first 5 ingredients into a large bowl and mix together. In a separate bowl whisk together the remaining ingredients. Combine the two mixtures until well coated.

Spread in a single layer onto a 12 x 15 inch baking sheet with side rim. Bake in preheated oven for 30 minutes, stir every 10 minutes. Let cool completely before serving.

Store party mix in one or more air-tight containers.

Sweet and Salty Trail Mix

1/2 cup toasted coconut, shredded
2 cups puffed-rice cereal
1/2 cup sesame sticks
1 cup roasted pepitas
1 cup roasted peas
2 tablespoons unsalted butter
1 tablespoon ground ginger
2 tablespoons light-brown sugar
1/4 teaspoon salt

Preheat oven to 250 degrees F.

In a large mixing bowl stir together the first 5 ingredients. Melt the unsalted butter in a small saucepan over medium heat, once melted add the ginger and brown sugar. Heat until sugar is completely melted. Pour butter mixture over cereal mixture. Sprinkle with salt and using a wooden spoon toss until well coated.

Spread out in a single layer on a baking sheet with rimmed edges. Bake in preheated oven for 30 minutes. Let cool completely before serving.

Store trail mix in one or more air-tight containers.

New Orleans Party Mix

1/2 cup pecan halves, raw
1/2 cup whole almonds, raw
1/2 cup walnut halves, raw
1/4 cup sunflower seeds, shelled & unsalted
1/4 cup pumpkin seeds, shelled & unsalted
2 tablespoons canola oil
1/4 teaspoon sea salt or table salt
1/4 teaspoon chili powder
1/4 teaspoon garlic powder
1/4 teaspoon cayenne pepper
1/4 teaspoon cumin

Preheat oven to 350 degrees F.

In a large glass bowl, toss together all the above ingredients until completely coated. Spread the mixture out into a single layer on a baking sheet and bake for 15 minutes, stirring every 2 to 3 minutes. Once toasted let the party mix cool.

Store party mix in one or more air-tight containers.

Kiddo's Trail Mix

2 cups whole-grain cereal, low in sugar

1 cup dried cranberries or other dried fruit

1 cup nuts, chopped (any nuts will do)

1 cup sunflower seeds or pumpkin seeds, shelled

1 cup raisins

1 cup chocolate chips

Place all the ingredients into a large bowl and mix together with wooden spoon until well blended.

Store trail mix in one or more air-tight containers

Happy Holiday Party Mix

2 1/2 cups Cheerios

3/4 cup mini pretzels

1 cups salted mix nuts

2 1/2 cups Corn Chex

1 1/2 cups dried cranberries or white raisins

1 package (12 ounces) white chocolate baking chips

1 1/2 tablespoons canola oil

Place the first four ingredients into a large bowl and mix together. Pour canola oil and white chocolate chips into a microwave safe bowl and microwave at 70% power for one minute, stir once, then microwave on high for five seconds and stir again.

Pour over the cereal/nut mixture and blend well. Spread party mix over three baking sheets lined with parchment paper. Let cool then break apart; place in a large bowl and toss in the dried cranberries.

Store party mix in one or more air-tight containers.

Haunted Halloween Party Mix

2 cups Corn Chex
1/2 cup pumpkin seeds, shelled
2 cups air popped pop corn
1 cup cashews, honey roasted
3 tablespoons brown sugar, packed
1 tablespoon light corn syrup
1/3 cup butter
1/3 teaspoon vanilla
1/2 teaspoon sea salt (optional)
1/4 teaspoon pumpkin pie spice
1/2 to 3/4 cup candy corn or dried fruit

Place cereal, pumpkin seeds, popcorn and cashews into a 2 quart microwavable bowl; then set aside. In a separate bowl mix together the brown sugar, corn syrup, butter, vanilla and sea salt, place in microwave uncovered and cook on high for 1 minute, stir after the first 15 seconds.

Remove from microwave and stir in the pumpkin pie spice. Pour butter mixture over the dry mixture and stir well to coat evenly. Microwave on high for 2.5 to 3 minutes, stir and scrape sides of bowl after each minute.

Pour mixture onto a sheet of parchment paper and let cool for approximately 15 minutes. Once cooled, toss mixture to break it up. Stir in the candy corn or dried fruit.

Store party mix in one or more air-tight containers.

Lightning Source UK Ltd.
Milton Keynes UK
UKOW06f0243100216

268058UK00010B/127/P